NEW VANGUARD 214

# US HEAVY CRUISERS 1943–75

## Wartime and Post-war Classes

**MARK STILLE**                    ILLUSTRATED BY PAUL WRIGHT

First published in Great Britain in 2014 by Osprey Publishing,
PO Box 883, Oxford, OX1 9PL, UK
1385 Broadway, 5th Floor, New York, NY 10018, USA
Email: info@ospreypublishing.com

Osprey Publishing is part of Bloomsbury Publishing Plc

A CIP catalog record for this book is available from the British Library

Print ISBN: 978 1 78200 632 9
PDF eBook ISBN: 978 1 78200 633 6
ePub ISBN: 978 1 78200 634 3

Index by Fionbar Lyons
Typeset in Sabon and Myriad Pro
Originated by PDQ Media, Bungay, UK
Printed and bound in India by Replika Press Private Ltd.

19 20 21 22 23   10 9 8 7 6 5

Osprey Publishing is supporting the Woodland Trust, the UK's leading
woodland conservation charity, by funding the dedication of trees.

**www.ospreypublishing.com**

# CONTENTS

# US HEAVY CRUISERS 1943–75
## WARTIME AND POST-WAR CLASSES

### INTRODUCTION

This book examines all the US Navy heavy cruisers built during and after World War II. This includes the largest class of heavy cruisers ever built, the 14-ship Baltimore class. Of these, only seven were commissioned in time to see service during World War II, but the entire class saw service during the Cold War and several went on to have distinguished combat careers during the Korean War and even the Vietnam War. Two ships of this class were extensively modified into the world's first missile cruisers, before returning to serve as conventional gun cruisers, and another two finished their careers as missile cruisers after being rebuilt.

Closely related to the Baltimore class was the Oregon City class, which was comprised of three ships built to a modified design. These had virtually the same capabilities as the Baltimore class but were different enough to carry a new class name. The most powerful and largest heavy cruisers ever built were the three ships of the Des Moines class. These were designed around a rapid-fire 8in gun. One of these ships was not decommissioned until 1975, thus making it the last heavy cruiser to be active in any of the world's navies.

The Baltimore-class heavy cruisers were the most powerful ships of their type in the world when they began to reach fleet service in mid-1943. This July 1, 1943, view of the lead ship gives an impression of its capabilities, showing its powerful main battery, bristling antiaircraft battery, and full electronics suite. (US Navy via Real War Photos)

The US Navy's extensive wartime cruiser construction program also included provisions for a number of large cruisers to counter any super-cruisers thought to be under construction by the Axis powers. Two of these ships were completed and saw service during the war. As predicted by many at the time, these proved to be white elephants.

Readers interested in the heavy cruisers built prior to World War II are referred to New Vanguard 210 *US Heavy Cruisers 1941–45: Prewar Classes*, which details the construction and history of US Navy Treaty heavy cruisers.

*Baltimore* seen from the carrier *Yorktown* on April 14, 1944, just before operations to support the landing on Hollandia on New Guinea. With their high speed, great endurance, and heavy antiaircraft fit, *Baltimore* and her sisters were ideally suited for carrier-protection duties. (US Navy via Real War Photos)

## THE CHANGING ROLE OF THE HEAVY CRUISER

With an early war deficit of capital ships, the US Navy was forced to use heavy cruisers as its principal surface units in the fierce battles around Guadalcanal in 1942. During this grinding six-month battle of attrition, American heavy cruisers suffered heavily; of the 11 committed to surface engagements, all were sunk or damaged by the end of the campaign. In 1943 and for the remainder of the war, surviving and new heavy cruisers were limited to two major roles. The first was shore bombardment, for which their 8in guns were well suited, and the other was antiaircraft screening of carrier forces. Given their speed, modern radar, and antiaircraft fits, the new Baltimore-class heavy cruisers were always assigned to carrier-screening duties. On no occasion did they have the opportunity to engage Japanese naval units. Only one Baltimore-class unit saw action in the Atlantic theater, assigned to conduct shore bombardment in support of amphibious landings. At this point in the war, the air threat posed by the Germans was limited.

On March 19, 1945, *Pittsburgh* came to the assistance of the heavily damaged carrier *Franklin* when the latter was bombed off the coast of Kyushu. *Pittsburgh* rescued many crewmembers who had jumped into the water to escape the smoke and fire, and then successfully passed a towline to the carrier. She slowly pulled *Franklin* out of danger and twice beat off Japanese air attacks in the process. (US Navy via Real War Photos)

After the end of the war, the heavy cruiser found itself without a natural enemy. The main threats to the US Navy going into the Cold War came from Soviet submarines and air attack in the form of air-launched guided missiles. However, this is not to say that the heavy cruiser did not have a viable mission during the Cold War. While its main battery of 8in guns was designed primarily as an antisurface weapon, it was also ideally suited for shore

bombardment. This lesson was once again learned during the Korean and Vietnam Wars, and with battleships almost extinct, heavy cruisers were usually the heaviest weapons available for shore bombardment. In this role they proved highly effective, since they operated against minimal opposition and had the range and firepower to engage a variety of targets.

Heavy cruisers could be operated far more efficiently than a battleship. This meant that many were maintained in service, and as the largest US Navy combat ships afloat (except for carriers) their impressive size made them ideal for naval diplomacy missions and for service as fleet flagships. The three ships of the Des Moines class spent much of their careers rotating as the flagship of the Sixth Fleet in the Mediterranean, and several Baltimore-class ships were used as the Seventh Fleet flagship in Far Eastern waters.

Perhaps somewhat surprisingly in the era of antiship missiles, American heavy cruisers enjoyed a long life after World War II. The last of the breed was *Newport News*, which was sent to the Pacific in 1967 and served off Vietnam until 1972. In 1975 she was the last heavy cruiser to be decommissioned, which brought the era of American heavy cruisers to an end.

Most of the Baltimore-class ships that were retained in service spent most or all of their active careers in the Pacific. This March 1955 view of Naval Station Yokosuka in Japan makes that point. Visible are Baltimore-class ships *Helena*, *Toledo*, and *Los Angeles*, as well as the Oregon City-class ship *Rochester*, which can be identified by her single stack. The carrier is *Princeton*. (US Navy via Real War Photos)

## US NAVY WARTIME HEAVY CRUISER DESIGN

The last of the Treaty heavy cruisers was the unique *Wichita*. She was based on the 10,000-ton light cruisers of the Brooklyn class, but equipped with an 8in main battery. In general, the US Navy considered *Wichita* to be successful, but the 10,000-ton limit caused the design to be cramped and to exhibit stability problems. Nevertheless, it was successful enough to be used as the template for the next three classes of heavy cruisers.

The primary reason for the development of the heavy cruiser was to get a main battery of 8in guns to sea. The US Navy had a love–hate relationship with the 8in gun. The Treaty cruisers were given an 8in main battery because this was the largest gun allowed per Treaty restrictions, and because the heavier gun gave a longer range and greater penetrative power against armored targets than the existing 6in gun. Even before World War II there was concern with the performance of the 8in gun based on gunnery trials. More importantly, wartime experience showed that the 8in gun fired too slowly, mainly because it used bagged powder charges, which made for a longer reload cycle. Rate of fire was also decreased by the time required to move the barrel to a loading angle and then back to the proper angle to fire. The rate of fire for Treaty cruisers was three or four rounds per minute, which was too slow to engage fast-moving targets even with the use of radar. This was demonstrated during the Guadalcanal campaign when heavy cruisers were employed to engage Japanese destroyers, usually unsuccessfully, and they often suffered in the process. As a result, the heavy cruisers (those that survived) were moved out of the Solomons in 1943 and employed

in Aleutian waters or on fast carrier escort duties. In their place, the Cleveland-class cruisers with their fast-firing 6in guns (eight to ten rounds per minute) were employed in the Solomons. The need to remedy this problem prompted the US Navy to develop 8in guns that combined the long range of the 8in gun with the fast-firing capabilities of the 6in gun. This was the basis for the design of the Des Moines class, which was the last and most powerful US Navy heavy cruiser design.

The full extent of the issue with the 8in gun was unknown before World War II, as the US Navy was formulating its wartime construction plans. However, the worth of the heavy cruiser in the mind of American admirals relative to the light cruiser can be judged by the fact that many more

*Des Moines* was the lead ship in the largest and most powerful class of heavy cruisers ever built. At over 716ft long, she was larger than most World War II battleships. This is the ship with her crew manning the rails in December 1959. She was decommissioned less than two years later and saw no further service until scrapped in 2007. (US Navy via Real War Photos)

The Alaska-class large cruisers were beautiful and powerful ships, but had no real definable purpose. Though larger than any heavy cruisers, their cruiser lines are still discernible, which precluded carrying heavy armor, thus it is impossible to consider them true battlecruisers. This fine port-bow view of *Alaska* is from November 1944 while the ship was on trials. The cruiser is wearing the MS 32/1D dazzle camouflage scheme. (US Navy via Real War Photos)

Cleveland-class light cruisers were completed during the war than Baltimore-class heavy cruisers. In spite of this, construction of the Baltimore class had a prominent place in the wartime cruiser construction program. Since it was basically an enlarged version of *Wichita*, designers were able to address the stability problem, and leave room for future growth. The scale of protection for these ships was also increased. Ironically, in the end this meant the heavy cruiser had a much longer life than the light cruiser, which was too cramped to sustain the addition of postwar electronics and in some cases batteries of large antiair missiles.

The Alaska-class large cruisers were an anomaly, since they were built for a mission that did not exist. Entering the war in its last few months, they were never used in their intended role and never had their cruiser-like protection tested by enemy shells, torpedoes, or bombs. The fact that they were even built speaks more to the profligacy of the US Navy's wartime construction program than anything else.

## HEAVY CRUISER WEAPONS

The Baltimore-class ships were completed with the 8in/55 Mk 12 and 15 guns. *Baltimore* had the Mk 12/1 gun and the rest of the class had the Mk 15/0. These were solid weapons, which proved successful in service. They fired a 335lb armor-piercing shell or a 260lb high-explosive shell. The principal shortcoming of the weapon was a relatively slow rate of fire, although this was comparable to other 8in guns of the day. The US Navy's previous 8in guns had a dispersion problem, and the new 8in gun turret on the Baltimore class remedied this with individually sleeved weapons and by placing the guns farther apart.

In May 1943, the proposal was made for the development of a rapid-firing 8in gun. To achieve a rapid rate of fire, a brass cartridge case would be used with a sliding breechblock. This was the same technology used on the existing 6in/47 guns first used on the Brooklyn-class light cruisers. Another feature was that the guns could be loaded at any elevation, thus saving the time required to move the barrels back and forth to a loading position. It was not possible to get this gun in service before the end of the war, and the first weapons did not see service until 1948. Once available as the 8in/55 gun Mk 16, it worked well despite being very complex. It remained in service into the 1970s. It was never used against an enemy surface target, which the rapid-firing gun had been designed to engage. It remained a formidable weapon, firing a 335lb shell at the rate of up to ten rounds per minute.

The two forward 8in turrets on *Boston* in June 1944. These guns could throw a 335lb shell up to 30,000 yards. (US Navy via Real War Photos)

The Alaska-class large cruiser required a bigger main gun to successfully conduct its mission of destroying enemy heavy cruisers. To support this requirement, the US Navy developed a new 12in gun especially for the class. This entered service as the 12in/50 Mk 8/0. It fired a 1,140lb armor-piercing shell at a maximum range of over 38,000 yards giving it a theoretical range advantage of some 6,000 yards over Japanese heavy cruisers. The "super-heavy" projectiles gave better armor penetration performance between 20,000 and 30,000 yards than the larger 14in guns mounted on prewar battleships. The new mount encountered numerous problems in development, but these were rectified in service. Because of the need to develop this new weapon, and the low numbers produced, it was the most expensive US Navy gun mount produced during World War II.

The secondary gun of all wartime heavy and large cruisers was the proven 5in/38, which possessed fine accuracy and a high rate of fire. It is generally regarded as the finest dual-purpose naval gun of the war. Introduction of VT (proximity) fuzed shells in 1943 made them even more effective.

## Main and Secondary Guns

| Type | Muzzle Velocity | Max Range | Rate of fire |
| --- | --- | --- | --- |
| 8in/55 Mk 12 and 15 | 2,500ft/sec | 30,050yds | 3–4rds/min |
| 8in/55 Mk 16 | 2,500ft/sec | 30,050yds | 10rds/min |
| 12in/50 Mk 8/0 | 2,500ft/sec | 38,573yds | 2–3rds/min |
| 5in/38 | 2,600ft/sec | 18,200yds | 15–20rds/min |

A primary design consideration for the wartime classes of American heavy cruisers was to provide them with a robust antiaircraft capability. Treaty cruisers were found to be deficient in this area (as was every other type of prewar US Navy ship), and they were provided with extensive antiaircraft upgrades during the war. The Baltimore class incorporated these upgrades and added more capability. The most effective antiaircraft weapon was the aforementioned 5in/38 dual-purpose gun, which was mounted in six twin turrets on all war-built and -designed heavy cruisers. In the antiaircraft role, it could hurl a 54lb shell up to 27,400ft. It possessed a high rate of fire and used a modern radar-guided fire-control system.

Designers of the Baltimore-class ships used wartime experience to greatly upgrade the ships' medium-range antiaircraft weapons. To the maximum degree possible, 40mm quad mounts were fitted at the expense of lighter weapons. Providing these weapons with clear arcs of fire was an important design criterion. The 40mm quad mount was the most effective medium-range antiaircraft weapon of the war. Fire control was provided by the Mk 51 director, and the weapon proved effective out to about 3,000 yards. The standard short-range antiaircraft weapon aboard wartime heavy cruisers was the Swiss-

This photo was taken from *Baltimore* of a Japanese torpedo-plane attack on Task Force 58 on December 4, 1943. The aircraft has been hit by fire and is smoking slightly. Carrier escort was the main duty of Baltimore-class cruisers during the war. (US Navy via Real War Photos)

designed 20mm Oerlikon gun. This weapon was air-cooled, required no external power source, and was comparatively lightweight so it could be fitted in relatively large numbers aboard cruisers. It was originally fitted as only a single mount, but late in the war a twin mount was provided to increase firepower. The provision of the Mk 14 gun sight greatly increased its effectiveness, but this device needed external power. The 20mm Oerlikon was a last-ditch weapon only effective to a range of about 1,500 yards.

## Antiaircraft Guns

| Type | Muzzle Velocity | Max Range | Rate of Fire (theoretical) |
|---|---|---|---|
| 20mm Oerlikon | 2,740ft/sec | 4,800yds | 450 rds/min |
| 40mm Bofors | 2,890ft/sec | 11,000yds | 160 rds/min |
| 3in/50 Mk 22 | 2,700ft/sec | 14,600yds | 45–50 rds/min |

The kamikaze threat that debuted in late 1944 caught the US Navy by surprise. Aside from the 5in/38 gun, no other shipboard weapons fired a round big enough to stop a kamikaze plane. This forced the Navy to begin a crash program in order to develop an intermediate gun big enough to deal with the kamikaze threat, replacing the inadequate 40mm and 20mm guns. Ideally, the new weapon would have a high rate of fire and be big enough to handle the VT fuzed shell.

The standard 3in/50 Mk 22 already in service was chosen as a basis for development since it could be readily adapted for automatic fire and the gun fired a shell that could carry the VT proximity round. It was first tested in September 1945, but not introduced into the fleet until 1948 in any numbers. The twin mount was known as the Mk 27, and an improved mount was designated as the Mk 33. The result was a successful weapon, which was more effective against aerial targets at longer ranges. It could engage a target at up to 30,400ft with a 24lb VT shell. Though complex and requiring regular and precise service, it was reliable, and remained in the fleet until the 1990s.

## Radar

The US Navy used a confusing system for designating radars because the Bureau of Ordnance, responsible for fire-control radars, used the Mark system, and the Bureau of Ships, which was responsible for search radars, used a system of letters that denoted purpose and sequential modification. The standard fit for war-built cruisers was the SK air-search radar on the mainmast, which could detect a large target at up to 100 nautical miles flying at 10,000ft. Some ships received the SP radar on the mainmast, which had a maximum range of 50 nautical miles against a large, high-flying target. This was vitally important as it provided fairly accurate elevation accuracy, which was critical for providing fighter direction.

The mainstay surface-search radar was the SG radar. This was the first American microwave radar to incorporate a display, which made interpretation much easier. It first entered service in 1942, and the improved SG-1 entered service in May 1943. The SG radar was placed on the top of the foremast, with a second set on the mainmast for 360-degree coverage (though ships equipped with the SP radar only carried one SG set). Its theoretical maximum range was 22 nautical miles against a large surface target.

The fire-control radars fitted on US Navy heavy cruisers were of the highest order. For the main battery, the Mk 34 fire-control director was fitted

with the Mk 8 radar, which had a tracking range out to 40,000 yards on a large target with a range accuracy of 15 yards. The secondary battery was provided with the Mk 37 fire-control director and the Mk 12/22 radar combination. The Mk 12 radar had a tracking range out to 45,000 yards for a large aircraft and 40,000 yards on a large ship, with a tracking accuracy of 20 yards. The Mk 22 was a height-finding radar used to detect low-flying aircraft. The Mk 51 radar was provided for the 40mm battery, and this was replaced on some ships late in the war by the Mk 56, which also provided fire control for the 3in battery.

The pace of advancement for ship-borne electronics was quick in the postwar years, and heavy cruisers received several stages of modernization to their electronic suites. In the late 1940s, the SR-3 radar replaced the SK. In the 1950s, the SPS-6B was introduced for air search, and fitted on the foremast. This was the first postwar air-search radar and was first fitted on *Macon* in 1950. This was quickly replaced by the SPS-12 on many ships. The most modern surface-search radar was the SG-6, and the SPS-8A was placed on the mainmast for height finding.

Ships surviving into the late 1950s received another wave of modernization, which included the SPS-29 on the foremast for air search and the SPS-10 for surface search. The final radar introduced on a handful of units was the SPS-37, which had a large antenna fitted on the foremast. The SPS-37A was an improved version of the SPS-29 with a much larger antenna, which increased range. It was first installed on *Los Angeles* in 1960 for operational evaluation. In the early 1960s the advanced SPS-10 surface-search radar was fitted. The table below provides an overview of principal heavy-cruiser radars.

*St. Paul* taking fuel in May 1970. Note the final electronics fit, which includes the SPS-37A air-search radar on the foremast, SPS-12 (not visible on the mainmast), and SPS-10. Her 26 years of active service is a record for a US Navy gun-armed heavy cruiser. (US Navy via Real War Photos)

## Postwar Heavy Cruiser Radars

| Radar | Purpose | Maximum range |
|---|---|---|
| SPS-6A/B/C | Air search | 70–140 nautical miles (against large targets) |
| SPS-8A/B | Height-finding | 72 nautical miles (actual) |
| SPS-10 | Surface search | 8 nautical miles (vs. periscope-sized target) |
| SPS-12 | Air search | 75–90 nautical miles (actual) |
| SPS-29 | Air search | 270 nautical miles (theoretical) |
| SPS-37 | Air search | 233–300 nautical miles (actual) |

# THE HEAVY CRUISER CLASSES

## Baltimore class

### Design and Construction

The Baltimore class was the largest class of heavy cruisers ever built. The light cruiser contemporary of the Baltimore was the Cleveland class, which was the largest class of cruiser ever built. This was no accident and reflects the grandiose plans made by the US Navy in the build-up to America's entry into World War II. To get these huge numbers of cruisers into service as quickly as possible, existing designs were used as a basis for the new ships. Both the Baltimore and Cleveland classes can trace their origins back to the Brooklyn class of 10,000-ton light cruiser designed during the period when Treaty restrictions were in place.

The programmatic origin of the Baltimore class began in late 1939 when the General Board (a body of admirals responsible for developing and approving ship designs) proposed an improved Wichita-class design of 12,000 tons as part of the list of designs to augment cruiser numbers.

*Baltimore* on July 1, 1943, during the ship's work-ups. Note the two aircraft cranes, which were only fitted to the first four ships of the class. The two floatplanes are OS2U Kingfishers, which was the standard floatplane for the Baltimore class until late 1944. (US Navy via Real War Photos)

Baltimore was the first ship of her class to reach the combat zone in the Pacific. This November 20, 1943, view shows Baltimore in the foreground as American ships bombard Japanese targets on Makin in the Gilbert Islands. (US Navy via Real War Photos)

The Fiscal Year 1941 building program was augmented by the Two-Ocean Navy Act, with the result that eight of the new Baltimore-class heavy cruisers were funded. These were quickly seen as inadequate for wartime requirements. A plan taking into account actual US ship-building capabilities and the needs of the Navy was formulated in early 1942 and approved in August 1942. This included 16 additional heavy cruisers (CA122–CA138 (less CA134). Of these, four were built to a modified design (the Oregon City class), six were completed to the original Baltimore-class design, and another six Oregon City-class units were cancelled in August 1945.

The first four ships were ordered on July 1, 1940. All were built at the same yard – Bethlehem-Quincy. Even after this, the General Board continued to push for more protection, but this was rejected for fear that any design modification would slow production. The second batch of four ships was ordered from the same yard on September 9, 1940. Of the ships ordered during World War II, only six were ever finished, making a total of 14 Baltimore-class heavy cruisers. This was still easily the largest class of heavy cruiser ever built.

## Baltimore-class Construction

| Ship | Built at | Laid down | Launched | Commissioned |
|------|----------|-----------|----------|--------------|
| Baltimore (CA68) | Bethlehem, Quincy, Mass. | 26/5/41 | 28/7/42 | 15/4/43 |
| Boston (CA69) | Bethlehem, Quincy, Mass. | 31/6/41 | 26/8/42 | 30/6/43 |
| Canberra (CA70) | Bethlehem, Quincy, Mass. | 3/9/41 | 19/4/43 | 14/8/43 |
| Quincy (CA71) | Bethlehem, Quincy, Mass. | 9/10/41 | 23/6/43 | 15/12/43 |
| Pittsburgh (CA72) | Bethlehem, Quincy, Mass. | 3/2/43 | 22/2/44 | 10/10/44 |
| St. Paul (CA73) | Bethlehem, Quincy, Mass. | 3/2/43 | 16/9/44 | 17/2/45 |
| Columbus (CA74) | Bethlehem, Quincy, Mass. | 28/6/43 | 30/11/44 | 8/6/45 |
| Helena (CA75) | Bethlehem, Quincy, Mass. | 9/9/43 | 28/4/45 | 4/9/45 |
| Bremerton (CA130) | New York Shipbuilding | 1/2/43 | 2/7/44 | 29/4/45 |
| Fall River (CA131) | New York Shipbuilding | 12/4/43 | 13/8/44 | 1/7/45 |
| Macon (CA132) | New York Shipbuilding | 14/6/43 | 15/10/44 | 26/8/45 |
| Toledo (CA133) | New York Shipbuilding | 13/9/43 | 5/5/45 | 27/10/46 |
| Los Angeles (CA135) | Philadelphia Navy Yard | 28/7/43 | 20/8/44 | 22/7/45 |
| Chicago (CA136) | Philadelphia Navy Yard | 28/7/43 | 20/8/44 | 10/1/45 |

The actual design of the new class of heavy cruiser was the subject of some debate. Because the hull had a light-cruiser ancestry, the new design had a basic light-cruiser arrangement like on the Cleveland class. The General Board considered other larger and more complex designs for the new heavy cruiser, but these were rejected in favor of the modified Wichita-class design, which was deemed easier to produce. However, the General Board did insist on an increase in protection. The Board also recommended that displacement be increased by 500 tons to a total of 12,500 tons. The final selection of the

This view is from *Boston* as ships of the Third Fleet blast Japanese steel-production facilities at Kamaishi on the home island of Honshu on August 9, 1945. *Boston* and the other ships in her class never had an opportunity to engage surface targets during the war, but did conduct shore bombardment on several occasions. (US Navy via Real War Photos)

design was made on December 15, 1939. The displacement continued to grow, even after approval of the design. By the middle of 1940, the displacement had grown to 13,300 tons and length to 664ft at the waterline, with the extra weight due to a longer main belt and additional splinter protection topside.

The principal problem with the Wichita class was its poor stability, which was directly attributable to the 10,000-ton Treaty limit. While the Baltimore-class ships retained the basic layout and protective scheme of the *Wichita*, the new design was much larger. The hull was lengthened by some 65ft and the beam was increased by 9ft, which addressed the stability problem. Overall design displacement was increased from *Wichita*'s Treaty-derived 10,000 tons to 13,600 tons.

The arrangement of the machinery spaces reflected that of the Cleveland class. The four boilers generated 120,000 SHP, which translated to a top speed of 33 knots, which was just below the design speed of 34 knots. There were four boiler rooms instead of two in the original design, and this required another 16ft added to the overall length and another 500 tons of displacement. The boilers were more efficient high-pressure types (615lb per square inch at 850 degrees Fahrenheit) and each was placed in its own compartment. The forward pair of boilers was separated from the aft pair by the forward turbine compartment in what was called the unit principle. This was an advance compared to previous designs, which grouped all the boilers together, meaning that a single critical hit could knock out all propulsive power. The ship also received two diesel generators, which could provide back-up power in a damage-control scenario.

Protection was broadly similar to that on *Wichita*. The main belt remained at a maximum of 6in, but was extended forward to protect the plotting room and the central fire-control station from *Pittsburgh* on. The belt was tapered down to 4in on its lower edges, and was tapered to 3in (main belt) and

 **THE BALTIMORE CLASS**

The top two profiles are of *Pittsburgh* in her late-war configuration (November 1944). The ship is in its striking Measure 32/18D dazzle camouflage scheme, which was intended to complicate an enemy submarine's calculation of the camouflaged ship's identity and course. The only difference from the early ships in the class is the single crane on the fantail. The bottom view is of Baltimore-class cruiser *Helena*, showing her in a postwar configuration in 1957. The 40mm and 20mm guns are gone, and twin 3in/50 mounts are now fitted. A Regulus missile can be seen aft on its launching ramp. The electronics fit has been thoroughly modernized. In addition to several types of ECM gear (in the covered domes), the primary air-search radar is now the SPS-6B, with the SPS-10 surface-search radar on the modified foremast. An SPQ-2 is fitted on the mainmast to control the Regulus. Note that the aft Mk 34 director has been removed. The ship is in the postwar MS 27 light-gray camouflage scheme. This called for all vertical surfaces to be painted haze gray (5-H), but this was a different shade than the wartime light gray since it had a lower blue content.

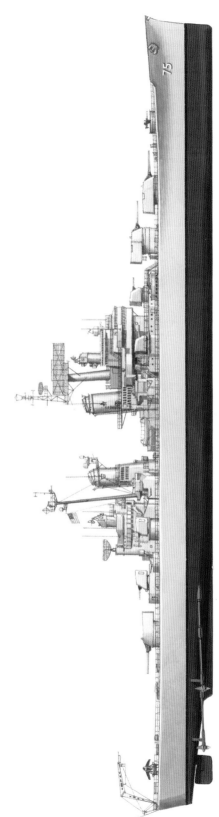

2in (lower belt) fore and aft of the machinery spaces. The armored deck was 2.5in in thickness, and the ends of the armored box were protected by bulkheads between 5–6in. Armor on the conning tower was removed from the first six ships to save weight and compensate for the growth of the antiaircraft battery. From *Columbus* on, the conning tower received 6.5in of armor on the sides, 3in on the top, 2.5in on the floor, and 2in on the tube.

The three 8in turrets were well protected with 8in of face armor, 3in on the roof, 3.25–1.5in on the side, and 1.5in on the rear. The six 5in/38 mounts also received some armor – 1in on the face and 0.75in on the sides and roof. The barbettes to the main battery received 6.3in of armor. Overall, the weight of armor was 1,790 tons, which equated to 12.9 percent of standard displacement. This indicated that the protective scheme of the Baltimore design did not receive as much additional protection as might be expected on a much larger hull compared to earlier heavy-cruiser designs.

For spotting and reconnaissance duties, it was still considered important to equip cruisers with aircraft. *Wichita* had her aircraft-handling facilities on the stern. This was favored for damage-control considerations and ease of operation, so the practice was continued on the Baltimore class. Two catapults were provided, and on the first four ships two aircraft cranes were placed on the fantail. After the first four ships, one of the cranes was landed, and the remaining one placed on the centerline on the fantail. There was also a small hangar on the stern, which could accommodate two aircraft. Overall, four aircraft could be carried.

### Armament

The main battery consisted of nine 8in Mk 12/15 guns placed into three triple turrets. As was now the custom on American heavy cruisers, two were placed forward with one in a superfiring position, and the third placed aft. Fire control for the 8in guns was provided by two Mk 34 directors, each equipped with a Mk 8 radar. One was placed forward and one aft. The secondary battery was to be similar to the Cleveland class – six twin 5in/38 mounts, all of which were enclosed. Fire control for these was provided by two Mk 37 directors equipped with the Mk 12/22 radar.

The light antiaircraft fit was modified from the original design, going from four 1.1in quad mounts to six 40mm quad and 12 single 20mm mounts. In July 1942 this was changed to four 40mm quad and 13 20mm mounts. This was clearly inadequate in light of wartime experience, so in December the two deleted 40mm quad mounts were restored and in February 1943 the number

A 1957 view of *Los Angeles*. The basic configuration of a Baltimore-class heavy cruiser remains unmistakable, but there have been some modifications. The 40mm quad mounts have been replaced by 3in/50 mounts and the radar fit has been modernized with the addition of an SPS-12 on the foremast and an SP on the mainmast. The ship is in the MS 27 light gray postwar camouflage scheme. (NARA)

of 20mm mounts was increased to 28. This was followed in June 1943 by a greatly improved allotment of 12 40mm quad mounts on the first four ships and 11 for the next four. The 12th 40mm quad mount on the first four ships was placed between the two aircraft cranes on the fantail. The next four carried only a single crane on the ship's centerline, so there was room to place two twin 40mm mounts on the fantail instead. In either case, the maximum number of 40mm guns carried was 48. Many of these mounts were placed in areas where they were susceptible to sea or blast damage. As soon as World War II was over, the forward three 40mm mounts were all removed. The number of 20mm single mounts going into production was set at 26.

Three-war veteran *St. Paul* pictured at anchor in Da Nang, South Vietnam, in May 1970. By this time, her armament had been reduced to ten 5in/38 guns (the forward 5in mount was removed as shown here to provide more office space for an embarked staff) and just six 3in/50 twin mounts, all amidships. (US Navy via Real War Photos)

## Wartime and Postwar Modifications

There was little modification made to the original designs, as it generally proved satisfactory and speed of production was deemed to be paramount. One important improvement was the installation of a Combat Information Center. This began on the first two ships as an enlarged radar plot behind the navigating bridge, then moved down to the main deck, but from *Pittsburgh* on it was placed below the main deck and protected by the armored belt.

In the 1950s, the quad 40mm mounts were replaced by 3in/50 antiaircraft guns in twin mounts. The usual number was ten twin mounts. These were controlled by four Mk 56 directors. The ships that did not see extensive service in the 1950s were not given 3in guns; *Quincy* retained 40mm mounts for her entire career. Ships that had Regulus surface-to-surface guided missiles installed lost a couple of 3in mounts so carried only a total of seven. Most ships which served into the 1960s retained only seven 3in mounts when retired.

The navigating and signal bridges were enclosed and the radar fit entirely upgraded as already outlined. The aircraft and catapults were removed, and since there was adequate space aft for a landing area, helicopters were embarked.

A little-known fact is that a Baltimore-class heavy cruiser was the first ship to possess the US Navy's sea-going nuclear deterrent when *Los Angeles*

## USS *BALTIMORE*

*Baltimore* as she appeared in April 1943 around the time of her commissioning. The ship was the lead unit in the largest heavy-cruiser class in naval history. When commissioned, *Baltimore* was the most powerful heavy cruiser in the world. She is in the MS 21 camouflage scheme, which was designed to minimize detection and identification by enemy aircraft.

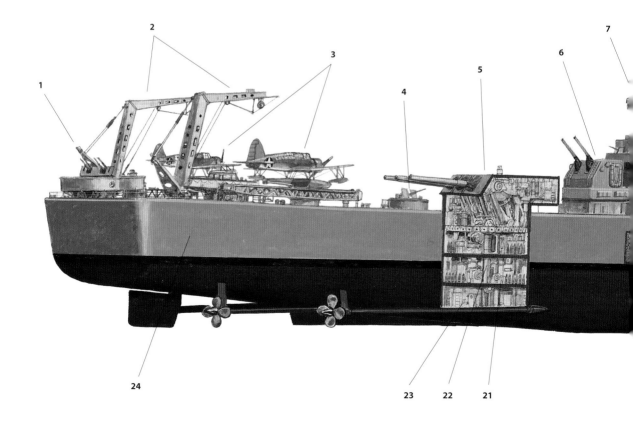

# KEY

1. Intermediate antiaircraft gun battery (12 40mm quad mounts)
2. Aircraft and boat cranes
3. Aircraft on catapults (two)
4. Light antiaircraft gun battery (26 single 20mm mounts)
5. Main battery (three triple 8in turrets)
6. Secondary battery (six twin 5in/38 mounts)
7. Mk 34 fire-control director with Mk 8/1 radar (two)
8. Mk 37 fire-control director with Mk 4 radar (two)
9. Mainmast
10. SG surface-search radar (two)
11. Secondary conning station
12. Stacks (two) each with two searchlights
13. Foremast
14. SK air-search radar
15. Combat information center
16. Pilot house
17. Flag plot
18. Forward boiler rooms (two)
19. Forward engine room
20. Aft boiler rooms (two)
21. Aft powder-handling room
22. Aft 8in turret barbette
23. Aft magazine
24. Aircraft hangar

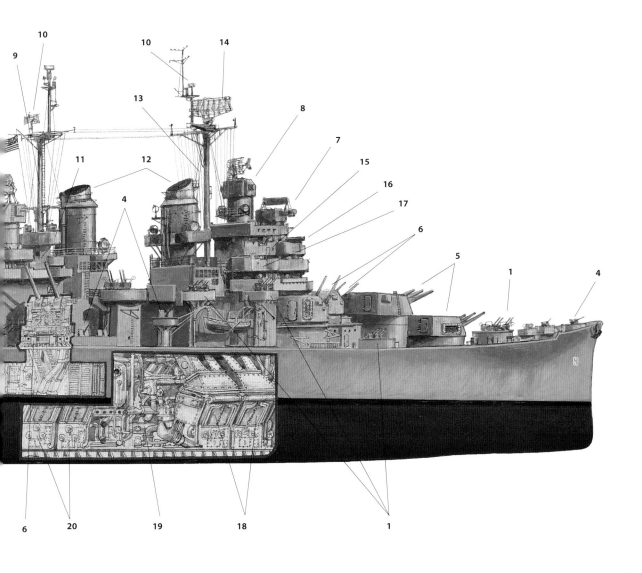

was equipped with the Regulus missile system in 1955. Regulus was powered by a turbojet and had a maximum speed of about 550 knots. The missile carried a single nuclear warhead. Range was intended to be 500 nautical miles, but was restricted in practice since the system had to be command guided, tracked, and steered by a platform within radio contact. Four cruisers – *Macon*, *Helena*, *Toledo*, and *Los Angeles* – were given the required launching ramps to use the weapon. These were fitted on the fantail. Three missiles were stored in the former aircraft hangar and the stern 3in gun sponsons were removed. The missile-control antenna placed on the mainmast was designated the SPQ-2 (a modified SP radar). With the advent of the sea-launched ballistic missile, the Regulus system was obsolete and was landed by the early 1960s.

After an 11-year rest, *Chicago* was selected for conversion into a guided-missile cruiser. This March 1978 view shows her refueling from USNS *Passumpsic* (T-AO-107). Her new configuration shows no sign of her heavy-cruiser heritage. (US Navy via Real War Photos)

*St. Paul*, *Helena*, and *Los Angeles* underwent limited conversion to serve as fleet flagships. This required the 5in mount in front of the bridge to be removed in order to provide more office space.

Several ships received extensive modifications to become missile cruisers. *Boston* and *Canberra* were converted to missile cruisers and recommissioned in 1955 and 1956, respectively. This was a basic modification that retained the existing cruiser characteristics forward and added two Terrier missile launchers and their associated electronics on the aft portion of the ship. Three additional ships – *Columbus*, *Albany*, and *Chicago* – were selected for a complete reconstruction as guided-missile cruisers. This was an extensive modernization that stripped the ships down to the main deck level. The result was an ungainly looking ship with tall masts and an array of electronics. The ships carried the long-range Talos surface-to-air missile (SAM) system fore and aft and the Tartar SAM system on the waist.

## Wartime and Postwar Service

Only seven Baltimore-class ships were completed in time to see service in World War II. The other seven were completed after the war, and most had relatively short service careers. Of the 14, nine were placed in reserve before the Korean War in 1950, and of these all but one (*Fall River*) saw service again.

*Baltimore* was the first ship to reach the combat zone. The ship only took 23 months to construct, a testimony to the efficiency of American shipbuilding. After a short shakedown, *Baltimore* reached the Pacific and was assigned to the Fast Carrier Task Force in time for the November 1943 invasion of the Gilberts. The cruiser was with the carriers for the February attack on the major Japanese base at Truk and then the invasion of the Marshalls in March. She remained with the carriers in April for the invasion of Hollandia on New Guinea. In June, the cruiser was part of the American force that decisively defeated the Japanese carrier force in June 1944 in the battle of the Philippine Sea. In July, *Baltimore* returned to the US west coast to embark

*Boston* seen in late November 1944, entering dry dock at an advanced base. The ship's MS 21 camouflage scheme is heavily worn, reflecting the fact that the cruiser had been operating virtually non-stop since January 1944. *Boston* was the most heavily decorated Baltimore-class ship of the war. (US Navy via Real War Photos)

Canberra as part of Task Group 38 on her way to conduct raids on airfields on Formosa, in a photo taken from the carrier Hornet on October 10, 1944. Three days later, she was hit by an air-launched Japanese torpedo, becoming the most heavily damaged Baltimore-class cruiser of the war. (US Navy via Real War Photos)

President Roosevelt and carry him to Hawaii to discuss the future of the Pacific War with Admiral Nimitz and General MacArthur. In August, the cruiser carried the President back to Alaska. Following an overhaul, it returned to carrier duty in November 1944 to cover the invasion of Luzon in the Philippines. Into 1945, *Baltimore* covered the invasion of Iwo Jima in February and spent June covering the invasion of Okinawa. For her wartime service, the ship earned nine battle stars. She remained in the Far East until February 1946 and was then decommissioned in July. In November 1951 the cruiser was recommissioned and assigned to the Atlantic Fleet. The ship conducted several deployments to the Mediterranean and represented the US at the 1953 Fleet Review in celebration of the coronation of Queen Elizabeth II. After being briefly transferred to the Pacific Fleet, the ship was decommissioned for the last time in May 1956. *Baltimore* was stricken from the Naval Vessel Register in February 1971 and sold for scrap.

*Boston* earned more battle stars (ten) than any of her sister ships for her wartime service. The cruiser joined the Fast Carrier Task Force in January 1944 and participated in the Marshalls invasion, the Hollandia operation, the battle of the Philippine Sea, the invasions of Saipan and Guam, and the battle of Leyte Gulf in October 1944, followed by the invasion of Luzon in January 1945. A March–June refit meant that the cruiser missed Iwo Jima and Okinawa, but *Boston* returned in time to take part in the final raids on Japan, during which she used her 8in guns to bombard the Japanese home islands. Upon returning to the US in March 1946, the ship was decommissioned. In January 1952 the cruiser was reclassified as a guided-missile cruiser and underwent a conversion

**C**  **USS *CANBERRA***

*Canberra* under attack by Japanese aircraft during the large-scale carrier raid on Japanese airfields on Formosa in October 1944. In this battle, *Canberra* was struck by a torpedo in her engine spaces. It was the most severe wartime damage suffered by any Baltimore-class cruiser. This scene shows the moment of the torpedo strike, with a backdrop of intense antiaircraft fire as the Japanese torpedo plane approaches its target. The Japanese also succeeded in torpedoing the light cruiser *Houston*. The Americans attempted to use the crippled cruisers to draw out portions of the Japanese fleet, but this gambit failed. Both cruisers were salvaged and returned to service. *Canberra* is in the MS 32/18D camouflage scheme.

*Canberra* entering a floating dry dock for maintenance in February 1944, before she joined the Fast Carrier Task Force. Note her fairly pristine MS 32/18D dazzle camouflage scheme. The large radar on the foremast is an SK. (US Navy via Real War Photos)

that was completed in November 1955. She served in this capacity until 1968, when the obsolescence of her missile system made the ship revert to its original purpose as an all-gun cruiser with her original hull number. She conducted three deployments to Vietnamese waters and was active in shore bombardments until being decommissioned in May 1970 after 28 years of service. The ship was stricken in 1974 and sold for scrap the following year.

*Canberra* had the distinction of being named for the Australian cruiser sunk at the battle of Savo Island in August 1942 as well as the dubious honor of being the Baltimore-class cruiser to suffer the most wartime damage. Her service began in February 1944 with operations in the last stages of the Marshall Island invasion. She remained with the carriers through Philippine Sea and into the raids on the Philippines, in preparation for the invasion of Leyte. While covering the raids on Formosa, the ship was struck by a Japanese air-launched torpedo on October 13. The torpedo hit aft and flooded both engine rooms, killing 23 men. The survival of the ship looked uncertain since she was left without power less than 100 miles from Japanese-held Formosa. However, she survived a series of air attacks and was towed to the fleet anchorage at Ulithi before returning to the US for permanent repairs. *Canberra* was decommissioned in March 1947. In January 1952, *Canberra* joined *Boston* as the world's first guided-missile cruisers. Recommissioned in June 1956, the ship served in this capacity until her final decommissioning in February 1970. This included four deployments to Vietnam and a reversion to her original hull number in 1968. She was sold for scrap in 1978.

The only Baltimore-class cruiser to see combat in the Atlantic theater during World War II was *Quincy*. After commissioning in December 1943, the cruiser's first action was on D-Day off Utah Beach on June 6, 1944. Later in June, *Quincy* engaged German shore batteries defending the key port of Cherbourg. In August, *Quincy* supported the invasion of southern France. In 1945, the cruiser embarked President Roosevelt and delivered him to Malta on his way to the Yalta Conference in February. *Quincy* returned the President to the US in February 1945. By April she joined the fast carriers off Okinawa. In May and July the cruiser took part in raids on Japan, earning the last of four battle stars. Upon returning to the US, *Quincy* was decommissioned in October 1946. In January 1952 she was briefly recommissioned for service off Korea, but was decommissioned for the last time in July 1954. *Quincy* was stricken in 1973 and sold for scrap the following year.

*Pittsburgh* earned two battle stars for her service off Iwo Jima in February and Okinawa from April to June 1945. During both campaigns, she engaged targets ashore. The ship also gave distinguished service protecting the crippled carrier *Franklin* after it was severely damaged on March 19 south of Kyushu. Though not damaged by the Japanese, *Pittsburgh* proved unable to escape from a major typhoon on June 5. The reported 100ft waves created pressures sufficient to knock the bow off as far as the Number 1 8in turret. None of the crew were lost, and the ship was able to return to the US for repairs. The ship was decommissioned in March 1947, but in response to the Korean War was brought back into service in September 1951. From 1952–54 she conducted three Mediterranean deployments and a cruise to the Indian Ocean. Her final deployment was as part of the Pacific Fleet from late 1954 into early 1955, which included operations in reaction to tensions in the Taiwan Strait between Communist China and the Nationalist government on Taiwan. She was decommissioned for the second and last time in August 1956. *Pittsburgh* was stricken in 1973 and then scrapped.

*Pittsburgh* suffered severe damage during a typhoon on June 5, 1945, when her bow broke off in front of the forward 8in turret. The crew was able to avoid the drifting bow and shore the exposed bulkheads. The ship arrived in Guam on June 10 without having lost a single man during this episode. (NARA via Robert Hanshew)

**RIGHT**
With a false bow, *Pittsburgh* departed Guam on June 24 and headed for the west coast of the United States for permanent repairs. The war ended before these were completed. (NARA via Robert Hanshew)

The only American heavy cruiser to see service in three wars was *St. Paul*. The cruiser arrived in the Pacific in July 1945 and took part in the final raids on Japan. These operations included bombardments of targets on the home islands. After the Japanese surrender, *St. Paul* was one of the few heavy cruisers maintained in continual commission. When the Korean War started, *St. Paul* was deployed to the Taiwan Strait to prevent hostilities from flaring up there. In November 1950 she deployed to the combat zone, where she provided carrier escort and conducted shore bombardment. After a brief refit in 1951 she returned to the waters off Korea, and in April 1952 suffered a fire in her forward 8in turret that killed 30 crewmen. The cruiser conducted a third deployment to Korea before the end of hostilities, and reportedly fired the last naval salvo of the war. She remained active in the Far East conducting another five deployments to the western Pacific before being the first ship permanently assigned to an overseas homeport (Yokosuka) for 39 months beginning in May 1959. From 1965–70 the cruiser conducted five additional western Pacific deployments, including gunfire support off Vietnam. In April 1971 she was decommissioned after just over 26 years of service. She was stricken in 1978 and scrapped in 1980.

*Columbus* enjoyed a long career since she was one of the two Baltimore-class cruisers selected for conversion into a missile cruiser. Her career began in June 1945, and she was one of the few kept in commission during the postwar drawdown. She participated in occupation duties in the Far East until being transferred to the Atlantic Fleet in 1948. Here she remained until 1955, and the cruiser made several deployments, including one to assume the duties as Sixth Fleet flagship. After returning to the Pacific, she made two western Pacific deployments until being decommissioned in May 1959 for conversion into a missile cruiser. After being recommissioned in 1962, the cruiser spent the rest of her career assigned to the Atlantic Fleet, and made seven Mediterranean deployments. In 1975 she was decommissioned, was stricken the following year, and sold for scrap in 1977.

*Helena* was commissioned in September 1945, thus missing the final stages of the Pacific War, but spent almost 18 years on continual service, nearly all with the Pacific Fleet. This included three wartime deployments to Korean waters, and several occasions operating in the vicinity of Taiwan during tensions between the Nationalists and Communists. The ship was decommissioned in 1963, stricken in 1974, and sold for scrap the same year.

*Bremerton* was commissioned in April 1945, but did not reach the Pacific until December. She was decommissioned in April 1948. In November 1951 she was brought back into service in response to the Korean War and conducted two wartime deployments to Korean waters. She remained active until 1960, conducting several additional western Pacific deployments before being placed in reserve again in July 1960. *Bremerton* was stricken in 1973 and sold for scrap the following year.

*Columbus* pictured in Malta's Grand Harbour in January 1949. From 1948 until 1955, *Columbus* served as flagship of several American and Allied naval commands in the Atlantic and Mediterranean, and this type of port visit was an integral part of her duties. (NARA)

*Helena* shown in September 1945, the same month she was commissioned. The ship is in the Navy blue MS 21 camouflage scheme. She was one of the few Baltimore-class ships to remain in commission after the drawdown following the war, and remained in service for the next 18 years, all in the Pacific. (US Navy via Real War Photos)

*Fall River* was not commissioned until July 1945, and thus missed the war against the Japanese. In 1946 she was used as flagship for the atomic test on Bikini Atoll. She conducted one cruise to the western Pacific before being decommissioned in October 1947. For the next 24 years she remained in reserve until being stricken in 1971, before being sold for scrap the following year.

*Macon* was commissioned in the waning days of World War II and did not see action in the Pacific. She remained active until 1950 on test and training duties before being placed in reserve in April of that year. She was quickly brought back into service in October and assigned to the Atlantic Fleet, and she conducted yearly deployments to the Mediterranean until 1959. She was placed in reserve in March 1961, and stricken in 1969.

*Toledo* served continually in the active fleet from her commissioning in October 1946 until being placed in reserve in May 1960. After an around-the-world cruise, she was assigned to the Pacific Fleet in June 1947 and remained there for her entire career. During this time she operated in the Taiwan Strait in 1948, and was one of the first American naval ships to intervene in the Korean conflict in July 1950. This was followed by two additional wartime deployments to Korean waters. During her career, *Toledo* made over ten western Pacific deployments, until being decommissioned in May 1960. The cruiser was stricken in 1974 and sold for scrap.

*Bremerton* had a fairly brief and typical career for a Baltimore-class ship, and did not enter service until after World War II. After a brief period of postwar service, she was reactivated in response to the Korean conflict and served the rest of her career in the Pacific. Here she is in September 1954 in Yokosuka, Japan. The carrier is *Point Cruz*. (US Navy via Real War Photos)

*Los Angeles* was another Baltimore-class Cold War warrior. Commissioned just before the end of the war, she did not see combat service in the Pacific. In April 1947, she was placed in reserve. In response to the Korean crisis, the ship was recommissioned in January 1951 and made two combat deployments to Korean waters, where she was lightly damaged by shore batteries in 1953. She remained in service until November 1963 and made a total of eight deployments to the western Pacific. She was stricken in 1974.

*Chicago* was named after the Treaty cruiser of the same name lost in January 1943. The new *Chicago* was commissioned in January 1945 and joined the fleet in time to participate in the last raids against Japan, during which she bombarded targets on the home islands. After a short period assigned to occupation duties in the Far East, she was decommissioned in June 1947. In November 1958, the cruiser was selected for conversion into a missile cruiser. This extensive work began in 1959 and was not finished until May 1964. In this new capacity she served

*Macon* in 1951 shows the typical modifications to a Baltimore-class ship that remained in service into the 1950s. Note that the three forward 40mm quad-mount positions have been vacated and the electronics fit has been modernized with the fitting of the SPS-6B air-search radar on the foremast. A temporary helicopter pad has been added aft. (US Navy via Real War Photos)

The standard intermediate-range antiaircraft weapon aboard all war-built heavy cruisers was the 40mm quad mount. This mount is shown aboard *Toledo* during the invasion of Inchon, Korea, in 1950. These were replaced by the more effective 3in/50 twin mount on almost all cruisers. (US Navy via Real War Photos)

Chicago was commissioned in time to get into action for the last few months of the war. Here the ship is shown in 1945 after commissioning, in the MS 21 camouflage scheme. She was decommissioned after only two and a half years as a heavy cruiser. (US Navy via Real War Photos)

until 1980, during which time she made nine western Pacific deployments including five combat deployments to Vietnamese waters. During one of these, she used her long-range missiles to destroy North Vietnamese aircraft. She was sold for scrap in 1991.

## Baltimore-class Specifications

Displacement: 13,600 tons standard displacement (design); 14,472 tons standard displacement (actual); 17,031 tons full load

Dimensions: length 673ft, 5in overall; beam 70ft 10in; draft 24ft.

Speed: 33 knots

Range: 7,900 nautical miles at 15 knots (actual); design 10,000 nautical miles at 15 knots

Crew: 1,426; rising to 2,039 in wartime

## Alaska class

### Design and construction

The Alaska class of large cruisers was the US Navy's attempt to build a super cruiser, not a battlecruiser as is often cited. The basic premise was to build a large cruiser able to run down and engage traditional heavy cruisers. Several foreign powers were rumored to be building super cruisers, including the Japanese. Even if the Japanese were not building super cruisers, it was known that their heavy cruiser force posed a threat. Japanese cruisers acting as commerce raiders posed a threat to American supply lines and also possessed the speed to track down and engage American carrier task forces, which would have only heavy cruisers as escort. This was the driving, if flawed, reasoning behind the design of the Alaska class.

 **ALASKA AND BOSTON CLASSES**

The top profiles show Alaska as she appeared in 1944 after joining the Pacific Fleet for the final drive on Japan. The ship maintains its basic cruiser configuration, with the main battery in three triple turrets and six 5in/38 mounts. The heavy antiaircraft armament includes 14 40mm quad mounts. The bottom profile depicts Boston in 1956 after being converted from a Baltimore-class heavy cruiser into a guided-missile cruiser. The ship kept her cruiser configuration forward, with six 8in guns and five twin 5in/38 mounts. Originally, six 3in/50 mounts were retained, but this was reduced to four in 1957. Aft are two Terrier Mk 10 double-armed surface-to-air missile launchers. Note that the two stacks have been trunked into one, and the entirely new electronics fit. The prominent radars aft are the two SPG-55B sets to provide fire control for the Terrier missiles.

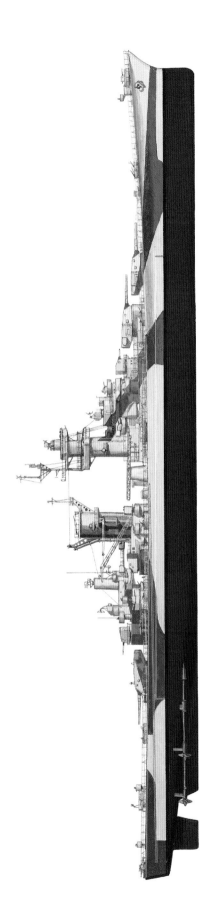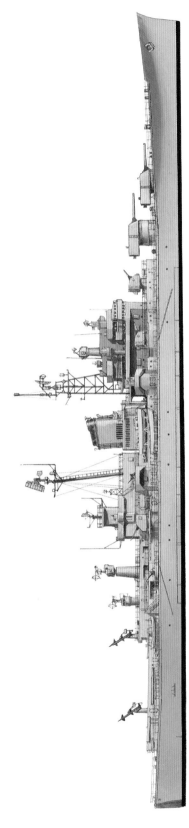

This starboard bow view of *Alaska* was taken in November 1944. The MS 32 camouflage scheme is effective in making it difficult to distinguish details, but her cruiser armament layout is obvious, with two centerline 5in/38 mounts. The quarterdeck is filled with antiaircraft weapons since the aircraft-handling facilities have been moved to an amidships location. (US Navy via Real War Photos)

In the end, the threat from Japanese super cruisers was non-existent and the threat from their heavy cruisers was overplayed. Ultimately, the Alaskas were seen as white elephants with no real purpose. The original proponent of the idea in 1938 was President Roosevelt, who liked to dabble in naval affairs. However, the concept cannot be dismissed as just the idea of a naval amateur, since Admiral Ernest King supported the idea when he was the commander of the fleet carrier force, as chairman of the General Board, and then as Chief of Naval Operations.

Deciding on the design of these controversial ships was an arduous process. The General Board considered several designs before settling on one with 12in guns and the protection to withstand 8in cruiser gunfire. The ship was designed with detached operations in mind. In the end, they were extremely expensive ships to fulfill what was essentially a cruiser mission.

The same General Board proposal in late 1939 that led to the Baltimore class also included a 26,000-ton design for a large cruiser. The following year, the General Board had become skeptical of the utility of a large cruiser design in light of the lack of construction by the Axis powers of high-speed capital ships, and they assessed that construction of large cruisers would not be a wise investment from a cost or time standpoint, especially as other types of ships were more urgently required.

The original four large cruisers were increased to six as part of the FY 1941 program, as augmented by the Two-Ocean Navy Act. The ships were ordered on September 9, 1940, from the New York Shipbuilding Corporation. In April 1942 the building program was cut back to only two large cruisers in favor of using available steel for the construction of destroyer escorts. In May 1943 the construction of four Cleveland-class light cruisers was cancelled and the deferred *Hawaii* was reinstated. At the same time, the last three Alaska-class ships were moved from a deferred status to canceled on June 24, 1943.

The names of the class give an indication of its intermediate position between heavy cruisers and battleships. They were named after territories, not states as in the case of battleships, or cities in the case of cruisers. The ships were designated CB, or large cruiser. They were not battlecruisers, as many writers have taken the CB to mean.

### Alaska-class Construction

| Ship | Built at | Laid down | Launched | Commissioned |
|------|----------|-----------|----------|--------------|
| *Alaska* (CB1) | New York Shipbuilding | 17/12/41 | 15/8/43 | 17/6/44 |
| *Guam* (CB2) | New York Shipbuilding | 2/2/42 | 12/11/43 | 17/9/44 |
| *Hawaii* (CB3) | New York Shipbuilding | 20/12/43 | 3/11/45 | Never |
| *Philippines* (CB4) | New York Shipbuilding | Not laid down – cancelled 24/6/43 | | |
| *Puerto Rico* (CB5) | New York Shipbuilding | Not laid down – cancelled 24/6/43 | | |
| *Samoa* (CB6) | New York Shipbuilding | Not laid down – cancelled 24/6/43 | | |

The Alaska design was not limited or influenced in any way by Treaty restrictions. This allowed designers to pay particular attention to improving protection. The resulting scale of protection was impressive for a cruiser, but not comparable to a fast battleship (which is what the battlecruiser had turned into). The main belt was 9.5in thick and was inclined at 10 degrees, which was unusual for a cruiser. The belt tapered down to 5in on its bottom edge. This was adequate to protect the machinery and magazines spaces from up to 12in shells at extended ranges. Horizontal protection was also fairly impressive, with a bomb deck of 1.4in and a main armored deck of between 2.8in inboard and 3.25in outboard. The armored bulkhead on each end of the armored box was 10.6in thick. The 12in turrets received 12.8in of armor on their face, 5in on their roof, between 6in and 5.25in on the sides, and 5.25in of armor in the rear. The barbette was armored with between 11in and 13in of armor. The conning tower was also armored and received a maximum of 9in. The total weight of armor was 4,720 tons, which amounted to some 16.4 percent of displacement. This was again comparable to a cruiser's level of protection, but far from that of a fast battleship. Because of her cruiser hull, no torpedo bulges were fitted, making the ships potentially vulnerable to torpedo damage.

The aircraft handling facilities were moved from the fantail to amidships. This had the advantage of increasing the height of the catapult, thus allowing aircraft to be launched in heavier weather, and it also moved the aircraft out of the blast of the ship's own guns. The location of the aircraft-handling facilities clearly showed the cruiser heritage of the design.

On trials in November 1944, *Alaska* recorded 32.7 knots on 154,846 SHP. This was disappointing since it was several knots below her design speed, and it meant that the ships had no potential speed advantage over an enemy cruiser.

*Alaska* recovers one of her floatplanes in Leyte Gulf in June 1945. The aircraft is a Curtiss "Seahawk" SC-1, which began to slowly replace the Kingfishers in October 1944. Unlike the aircraft handling facilities on Baltimore-class heavy cruisers, which were on the stern, the Alaska class carried its aircraft crane amidships, as seen in this view. (US Navy via Real War Photos)

It is not generally realized that *Alaska* arrived in the Pacific in time to see extensive service, for which she earned three battle stars. The great majority of this time was spent on carrier-escort duty, with the exception of a brief sortie into the East China Sea as part of a surface action group. This is a view from *Alaska* on March 18, 1945, as her antiaircraft batteries destroy a Japanese bomber headed for the carrier USS *Intrepid*. (US Navy via Real War Photos)

It was soon discovered that the pilothouse was too cramped, and that space for the flag bridge and flag plot was inadequate even though the ships were intended to act as flagships. More importantly, the ships' tactical diameter was excessive, making them hard to maneuver.

## Armament

The main armament of these large cruisers was the new 12in/50 gun developed specifically for this class. The ship was fitted with three triple turrets, giving it a broadside of nine 12in guns. The weight of a triple 12in turret with its armor was a considerable 930 tons. The fire-control director for the main battery had to be mounted higher than on the 8in gun cruisers to fully exploit the range of the 12in guns. Accordingly, the Mk 34 director was placed on top of the forward superstructure, in the style of US Navy battleships.

Secondary armament was identical to the modern heavy cruisers with six twin 5in/38 mounts with two on each beam and two on the centerline. The light antiaircraft armament was considerably augmented before completion. Originally, six quad 1.1in mounts were envisioned. This was converted to six 40mm quad mounts in May 1941. By August 1945, the light antiaircraft fit had been scaled up to 14 40mm quad mounts and 34 single 20mm guns. The ships were not modified during their short careers.

## Wartime Service

The lead ship of the class did not join the fleet until January 1945. By this point in World War II there was virtually no surface threat posed by the Imperial Navy, so the large cruisers never had an opportunity to function in the role for which they had been designed. Instead, they were assigned to the Fast Carrier Task Force and used as carrier escorts. In this role they performed well, since they possessed sufficient speed to keep up with the carriers and possessed significant antiaircraft capabilities.

*Alaska* spent the last seven months of the war on carrier-escort duty. She participated in the invasions of Iwo Jima and Okinawa and the carrier raids on the Japanese home islands. She used her 12in guns to bombard shore targets on Okinawa, and between July 16 and August 7 she operated in the East China Sea. For this service, she received a total of three battle stars. After the war she briefly remained in the Far East, supporting the occupation of Japan, Korea, and China, but by December 1945 had returned to the US. In February 1947, she was decommissioned and placed in reserve.

**E** **THE OREGON CITY CLASS**
These profiles depict *Rochester* in December 1946, when she was commissioned. This class of three ships was a modified Baltimore-class design, but was completed too late to see war service. The primary difference from the earlier class was the single stack. A more subtle difference was the different placement of main and secondary fire-control directors, with the Mk 37 director for the 5in battery situated over the conning tower and the Mk 34 main-battery director placed on top of the bridge superstructure. Otherwise, the armament layout and hull form were identical to the Baltimore class.

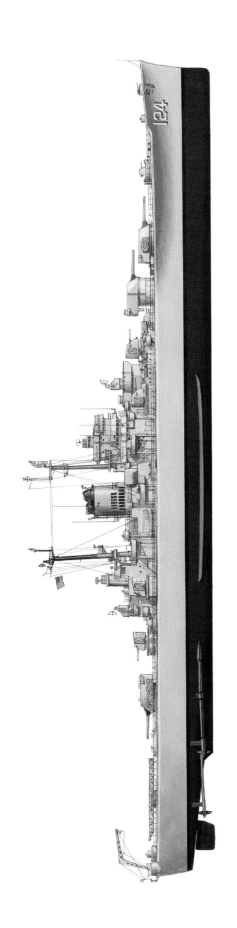

This view of *Guam* was taken while the ship was working up near Trinidad shortly after being commissioned in September 1944. The ship is in the dazzle MS 32/7C camouflage scheme, which she wore until 1945. She arrived in the Pacific in February 1945 and began combat operations the next month. (US Navy via Real War Photos)

The ship was never recommissioned, and was sold for scrap in 1961.

*Guam* earned only two battle stars, since she arrived in Pearl Harbor in February 1945 and joined the carriers in March. That month, she participated in the raids on Kyushu and Shikoku in preparation for the invasion of Okinawa. After a sortie into the East China Sea in mid-July to early August, she returned to Okinawa. After the war, she supported the occupation of Korea and returned to the US in November. The ship was decommissioned in February 1947, never to be brought back into service, and was sold for scrap in 1961.

The third ship in the Alaska class, *Hawaii*, was never finished. When World War II ended she was 84 percent completed, but construction was suspended. Her size and speed made her a candidate for conversion into a command ship or as a platform for guided missiles, but nothing ever came to fruition. She was finally sold for scrap in 1959.

### Alaska-class Specifications
Displacement: 29,779 tons standard displacement; 34,253 tons full load
Dimensions: length 808ft 6in overall; beam 91ft 1in; draft 31ft 10in
Speed: 33 knots
Range: 12,000 nautical miles at 15 knots
Crew: 1,517

## Oregon City class
### Design and construction
The design of the three Oregon City ships reflected wartime experience and the need to further simplify production. By November 1942, these changes were approved. Some were incorporated into the Baltimore-class ships still under construction. These modifications generally followed those planned for the follow-on to the Cleveland-class light cruisers. The first three ships of the

A fine port bow shot of *Oregon City*. The cruiser was launched just before the end of World War II but was not commissioned until February 1946. Her total career was the shortest of any war-built US Navy cruiser, since she was decommissioned in December 1947 and she never returned to service. (US Navy via Real War Photos)

Oregon City class were completed as heavy cruisers, and a fourth, *Northampton*, was completed after the war as a fleet flagship. Another six were all given names but were cancelled in August 1945.

## Oregon City-class Construction

| Ship | Built at | Laid down | Launched | Commissioned |
|------|----------|-----------|----------|--------------|
| *Oregon City* (CA122) | Bethlehem, Quincy, Mass. | 8/4/44 | 9/6/45 | 16/2/46 |
| *Albany* (CA123) | Bethlehem, Quincy, Mass. | 6/5/44 | 30/6/45 | 11/6/46 |
| *Rochester* (CA124) | Bethlehem, Quincy, Mass. | 29/5/44 | 28/8/45 | 20/12/46 |
| *Northampton* (CA125) | Bethlehem, Quincy, Mass. | 31/8/44 | 27/1/51 | 7/3/53 |
| *Cambridge* (CA126) | Bethlehem, Quincy, Mass. | 16/12/44 | Not launched – cancelled 12/8/45 | |
| *Bridgeport* (CA127) | Bethlehem, Quincy, Mass. | 13/1/45 | Not launched – cancelled 12/8/45 | |
| *Kansas City* (CA128) | | Not laid down – cancelled 12/8/45 | | |
| *Tulsa* (CA129) | | Not laid down – cancelled 12/8/45 | | |
| *Norfolk* (CA137) | Philadelphia Navy Yard | 27/12/44 | Not launched – cancelled 12/8/45 | |
| *Scranton* (CA138) | Philadelphia Navy Yard | 27/12/44 | Not launched – cancelled 12/8/45 | |

The only real difference from the Baltimore class was the trunking of the two stacks into one. This decreased top weight and created better arcs of fire for the antiaircraft suite. The height of the aft superstructure was also decreased for the same reasons. The locations of the main and secondary fire directors were interchanged. Like on the later ships of the Baltimore class, only one aircraft crane was fitted.

The Oregon City class was dimensionally identical to the Baltimore class, though the modified ships did have a slightly greater displacement. Protection and machinery was also the same.

### Armament and Service Modifications

The Oregon City-class ships had the same armament as the Baltimore class. Modification of this class generally followed those Baltimore-class ships retained in service postwar. *Oregon City* had none since she was only active for 22 months. She retained her original 12 40mm quad mounts throughout her short career. *Albany* was modernized before 1950 with the 3in/50 twin mounts replacing the 40mm quads. The number of mounts was reduced to eight. She was completed with two catapults, but these had been removed by 1950. Early in her career the SR-3 radar replaced the SK-2, and her final radars were the SPS-12 and the SPS-8A. The cruiser also gained six Mk 56 directors when the 3in/50 mounts were added. In 1957, *Albany* began

*Albany* pictured in mid-1946, probably during acceptance trials. She was completed too late to participate in combat operations, though she was destined to have the longest career of the three Oregon City-class ships. She is already in the light-gray MS 27 postwar camouflage scheme. The basic similarity to the Baltimore class is evident in this view, as is the single large stack, which is how the two classes were distinguished from each other. (US Navy via Real War Photos)

*Albany* experienced seven busy years in the heavy-cruiser role, and was then converted into a guided-missile cruiser and re-entered service in 1962. She served in this role for another 28 years until being decommissioned in 1980. These 35 years of active service make *Albany* the longest serving US Navy heavy cruiser. (US Navy via Real War Photos)

conversion into a guided-missile cruiser, the details of which are beyond the scope of this book.

*Rochester* followed a generally similar pattern to *Albany* but was completed with the SR-3 radar. In 1953, the 40mm quads were removed and replaced by a total of ten twin 3in/50 mounts. The catapults were removed in 1948. When decommissioned, she had the same electronics fit as *Albany* with the exception that one of the Mk 34 directors had been removed.

### Service Histories

*Oregon City* was placed in reserve in 1947, but the other two remained in service and were modernized. *Oregon City* was likely defective in some manner since she was decommissioned in December 1947 not even two years after completion, and was never recommissioned or converted. She was stricken in 1970 and scrapped in 1974.

*Albany* carried out a high operational tempo between 1949–56, making five Mediterranean deployments, as well as several cruises to the Caribbean, three to South America, and one to northern Europe. In 1957 she began conversion into a guided-missile cruiser, which took until 1962. The cruiser made six deployments to the Mediterranean until being permanently homeported in Italy from 1976–80. *Albany* was decommissioned in 1980, stricken in 1985, and sold for scrap in 1990.

*Rochester* entered service in December 1946 and made her first Mediterranean deployment in 1948. In early 1950 she was transferred to the Pacific Fleet and quickly responded to the North Korean invasion in June 1950. The cruiser spent 198 days off the Korean coast and expended 3,265 8in and 2,339 5in shells in shore bombardments. After a refit, *Rochester* returned to Korea in late 1951. By the time she was decommissioned in August 1961, the ship had made a total of nine deployments to the western Pacific. After remaining in reserve, the ship was stricken in 1973 and sold for scrap the following year.

The fate of the fourth ship of the class, *Northampton*, is interesting and will be related here even though she was never completed as a heavy cruiser. The importance of dedicated command ships was clearly shown during World War II, so when future development of this concept was decided upon, the incomplete (56.2 percent) hull of *Northampton* was selected. Construction

**F** **THE DES MOINES CLASS**

This plate shows *Salem* in May 1949, when she was commissioned. The three ships of this class were the largest heavy cruisers ever built. The main visual difference from the two earlier classes is the very tall main director towers, but a close examination will reveal that the bridge structure was also modified. The main battery is comprised of three triple turrets with 8in/55 Mk 16 automatic guns. The secondary battery is identical in numbers and placement to the previous two classes. The antiaircraft battery is comprised of 12 mounts of automatic 3in/50 guns. When commissioned, the primary radars were the SR-3 and SP, but the latter was quickly replaced by the SPS-6B as shown here.

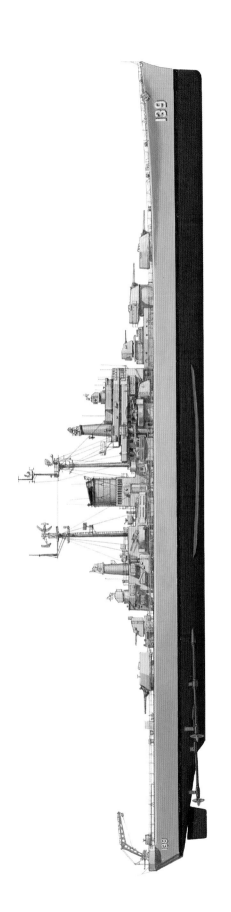

*Northampton* was originally a member of the Oregon City class of heavy cruisers, but was extensively modified and did not enter service until 1953. In this view, it is easy to discern her cruiser hull, but also to see that her new purpose is that of a command ship. The guns forward and aft are the fully automatic 5in/54 mounts. Note the profusion of communications equipment. (US Navy via Real War Photos)

was begun again in July 1948 to her new designation (CLC-1) as a command ship. It was envisioned that she could serve as a National Emergency Command Post Afloat for the President if need be. Accordingly, the ship was provided with a greatly augmented electronics-and-communications suite. The cruiser machinery and most of the armor was retained, but the armament was reduced to that required for self-protection (a combination of 5in and 3in guns). The ship entered service in 1953, was redesignated National Command Ship (CC-1) in 1963, and decommissioned in 1970. During her career, she served as flagship for the Sixth Fleet on several occasions, but was primarily dedicated as the flagship for Commander, Strike Force, Atlantic Fleet based out of Norfolk, Virginia.

### Oregon City-class Specifications

Displacement: 13,600 tons standard displacement (design); 14,472 tons standard displacement (actual); 17,031 tons full load
Dimensions: length 673ft, 5in overall; beam 70ft 10in; draft 24ft.
Speed: 33 knots
Range: 7,900 nautical miles at 15 knots (actual); design 10,000 nautical miles at 15 knots
Crew: 1,426; rising to 2,039 in wartime

## Des Moines class

### Design and construction

This beam view of *Salem* dating from June 1952 clearly shows the ship's layout. The primary distinguishing feature from the preceding Oregon City class were the two tall towers fore and aft, upon which the fire-control director for the main battery was placed. Otherwise, the single funnel, fantail aircraft-handling facilities, and weapons layout made it difficult to tell the classes apart. (US Navy via Real War Photos)

These were the largest heavy cruisers ever built. The new class was clearly superior to the earlier Baltimore and Oregon City ships. They were built around the new rapid-fire 8in gun, which offered the promise of increasing the rate of fire from the existing three rounds per minute to ten. It was originally hoped that the new weapon could be fitted on the Oregon City design, but the existing turrets could fit only a total of six 8in guns of the new type instead of the desired nine. This measure was rejected by the General Board in favor of a new, larger cruiser design that could also incorporate greater protection against torpedoes and bombs.

The new 8in guns required larger magazines to feed the faster-firing guns. In turn, this required that the main belt be extended to protect them. This created more weight and greater length. Overall length increased to 716ft and standard displacement grew to 16,900 tons. The ships' beam was just under 76ft, a significant increase from the previous class. At full load, the ships totaled just short of 21,000 tons, making them large ships by any measure.

The size of the program fluctuated with perceived wartime requirements and the limitations of cruiser-construction facilities. In June 1943, CA139 to CA142 were ordered to the new design from Bethlehem, and in October 1943, CA134 of the Oregon City class was re-ordered as a ship of the new class and construction transferred from New York Shipbuilding at Camden to Bethlehem. In addition to these five ships, orders for as many as seven more were placed before the approaching end of the war threw these plans into doubt. Four ships were cancelled in March 1945 and work on another three was suspended in August. These last three ships were also cancelled in late 1945, as was another in January 1946. This left four ships, which, if all were completed, would constitute a full cruiser division. Even this would not be realized, since in June 1946, CA140, now named *Dallas*, was cancelled because she was the least complete (7.8 percent) of the ships under construction.

## Des Moines-class Construction

| Ship | Built at | Laid down | Launched | Commissioned |
|---|---|---|---|---|
| *Des Moines* (CA134) | Bethlehem, Quincy, Mass. | 28/5/45 | 27/9/46 | 16/11/48 |
| *Salem* (CA139) | Bethlehem, Quincy, Mass. | 4/7/45 | 27/3/47 | 14/5/49 |
| *Dallas* (CA140) | Bethlehem, Quincy, Mass. | 15/10/45 | Never – cancelled 6/6/46 | |
| *Newport News* (CA148) | Newport News | 1/10/45 | 6/3/48 | 29/1/49 |

Despite a large increase in displacement and the retention of the standard 120,000 SHP four-shaft geared turbine machinery, the longer hull made it possible to achieve speeds of 32.5 knots during trials. The machinery was arranged in a unit configuration with each of the three forward machinery spaces containing a boiler and a turbine and the fourth machinery unit having separate boiler and turbine rooms. This increased the potential that damage would not cause a complete loss of power.

The much larger size and displacement meant that greater protection could be incorporated into the design. The thickness of the belt remained the same (6in tapering down to 4in with the belt being 10ft deep), but horizontal protection was enhanced with the provision of 1in armor on the weather deck to detonate both armor-piercing and high-explosive bombs before they reached the main deck armor of 3.5in (as opposed to 2.5in on the Baltimores). The turret barbettes were larger, costing an additional 255 tons to protect, and the thickness was 6.3in. The turrets themselves received another inch of armor on the roof, and another half inch on the rear and sides; this made the final total 8in on the face, 4in on the roof, 2–3.75in on the side, and 2in on the rear.

Another feature was the provision of four transverse armored bulkheads within the armored box. This was intended to stop the flooding within the armored box and keep the ship afloat even if the armor was penetrated. The position of the bulkheads was intended to keep the loss to a single 8in turret or one main machinery group after penetration by a bomb, shell, or torpedo. It was the first time this design was used on a heavy cruiser and was a major advancement.

Another 1951 view of *Newport News*. The layout of the secondary and antiaircraft batteries is clearly shown. Note the elevated positions of the 3in/50 mounts to give them better arcs of fire. (US Navy via Real War Photos)

Even as large as the new design was, the final design was changed by weight-saving requirements that forced a much smaller scale of protection. The bomb deck was reduced from 1in to 0.875in, the main armored bulkheads at either end of the armored box was reduced from 6in to 5in, and the internal bulkheads were reduced from the planned 2.5in to a mere 0.75in. Nevertheless, this was the best-protected heavy cruiser ever built, with a total weight of armor of 2,189 tons.

*Newport News* leads the carrier *Midway* into port at Athens, Greece, in March 1950. Note the helicopter on the fantail, which was by now standard equipment for all cruisers remaining in service. The positions of the 8in guns in the aft turret demonstrate that each gun could be elevated and fired individually. (US Navy via Real War Photos)

The class was designed with the typical two-fantail catapults and large aircraft crane. The lead ship was completed with catapults, but these were quickly removed. The other ships were not finished with catapults. The space on the fantail proved suitable for helicopter operations after the floatplanes were removed. The crane was retained and the hangar space used for the ship's boats.

Another new design feature was that *Salem* and *Newport News* were completed with prototype air-conditioning systems. *Des Moines* was never so equipped.

### Armament and Service Modifications

The new 8in rapid-fire gun was the driving reason behind the new class of cruisers. The new triple mount weighed in at a whopping 451 tons, not including the size of the barbette, which increased in size from 22ft 6in to almost 27ft. The extra weight of armor on the larger barbette was also considerable. The larger magazines also required a longer main belt to protect them. For these primary reasons, it was decided to wait for a new cruiser design rather than trying to adapt the Oregon City design for the new gun. The delay also permitted the development of a triple turret with the new gun instead of using a twin mount, in an effort to get the ship built earlier. When completed, the new class carried three triple turrets of the 8in/55 Mk 16 guns. For the first time on a cruiser, the main battery was provided with two separate plotting rooms. The main battery director was the new Mk 54, which replaced the standard Mk 34s. All range-finder gear was removed from turrets, since the provision of radar made them superfluous.

Secondary and antiaircraft armament remained as on the Oregon City class, with six twin 5in/38 mounts and 12 40mm quad mounts. However, the advent of kamikaze attacks changed the 40mm to the new twin 3in/50.

**G   USS *NEWPORT NEWS***

This scene shows *Newport News* conducting a bombardment of targets in North Vietnam in 1972. The cruiser is firing her main battery and is taking fire from North Vietnamese shore batteries. Also evident is the final configuration of the ship before being decommissioned in 1975. Among the changes is a different electronics fit, with the SPS-37 and SPS-10 on the foremast and the SPS-8A and SPS-6B on the mainmast. All 3in gun mounts have been removed and replaced by accommodations amidships for the embarked flag staff. Also indicative of her flagship duties are many additional communications antennae.

All ships were completed with 12 3in mounts and 12 20mm guns. The 20mm mounts were quickly removed due to personnel considerations, and the foremost 3in mount, which was susceptible to water damage, was removed in 1955. Two Mk 63 directors were provided for the aft mounts, and the rest were controlled by four Mk 56 directors. By 1963, *Newport News* had only eight 3in mounts, as did *Salem* and *Des Moines* when they went into reserve.

This fine starboard bow view of *Newport News* dates from September 1951. The ship is in the postwar MS 27 camouflage scheme. Note the full 3in/50 gun battery including two mounts forward of the forward 8in guns. The large radar on the foremast is the SPS-6B early warning radar. (US Navy via Real War Photos)

Two additional Mk 37 directors for the 5in mounts were fitted on the waist, bringing the total to four. This brought a considerable cost in deck space, but was considered essential. This was the same fit as on a battleship. The main battery directors could control the secondary battery, and vice versa, if required. A Mk 52 short-range director was provided for each 5in mount.

*Newport News* was rebuilt as a flagship in 1962. Two of the waist 3in mounts were removed and replaced with deckhouses, and the two forward 3in mounts were also removed, leaving her with eight. This was further reduced to four by 1966, and the last two had been removed by 1973. In their place was electronics and communication gear. Before being deployed to Vietnam, the ship received an array of electronic countermeasures equipment and chaff launchers to defeat the antiship cruise missiles in the hands of the North Vietnamese.

## Service Histories

All three ships were completed well after World War II, and only one was destined to have a long career. Because all were assigned to the Atlantic Fleet early in their life, none saw action in the Korean War.

During their early careers, their principal mission was to rotate to the Mediterranean, where they acted as flagships of the Sixth Fleet. They were ideally suited for this "presence" mission given their extra room for accommodating staff and their impressive size, making them visible instruments of American power in the region.

After nearly yearly deployments from 1949–1961, many to the Mediterranean, *Des Moines* was decommissioned in July 1961. The ship was not recommissioned and was finally stricken in July 1991. She remained at the Naval Inactive Ship Maintenance Facility in Philadelphia until 2006. After a failed attempt to turn her into a museum ship in Milwaukee, she was moved to Texas for scrapping, which was completed in 2007.

*Salem* had an even shorter life. The cruiser made seven Mediterranean deployments, but was taken out of service in January 1959. Despite a proposal in 1982 that she and *Des Moines* be reactivated as part of the build-up of the "600-ship Navy" of the Reagan era, it was judged that bringing the Iowa-class battleships back into service would be more effective. She never was recommissioned, and was stricken in July 1992.

*Salem* has the good fortune to be the only preserved heavy cruiser in the world. In 1994 she returned to the place of her birth in Quincy,

Massachusetts, where she became the centerpiece of the US Naval Shipbuilding Museum. She was opened to the public in May 1995, and remains there today.

*Newport News* had a prolonged career and served in both the Atlantic and Pacific Fleets. Between 1950 and 1961 she made multiple Mediterranean deployments. With the war in Vietnam ramping up, she moved to the Pacific Fleet in September 1967 and made the first of two deployments off Vietnam from October 1967 to April 1968 before returning to the Atlantic Fleet. In May 1972 she returned to the waters off Vietnam. On October 1, 1972, she was operating off the coast when an explosion occurred in the center gun barrel of Turret 2. All 16 men in the turret were killed, four additional crewmen died, and another 36 were wounded. Instead of replacing the turret with another from one of her sister ships, for cost reasons the center gun was removed and plated over, and the turret locked in the fore-and-aft position.

After two final deployments to northern Europe, the last heavy cruiser in US Navy service was decommissioned on June 27, 1975, and stricken three years later. She was sold for scrap in 1993.

This is *Salem* underway just after being commissioned. The ship served only ten years before being placed in reserve in 1959. Never recommissioned, she is the only heavy cruiser preserved anywhere in the world, and is on display in Quincy, Massachusetts. (US Navy via Real War Photos)

### Des Moines-class Specifications
Displacement: 17,531 tons standard displacement; 20,934 tons full load
Dimensions: length 716ft 6in overall; beam 75ft 4in; draft 26ft
Speed: 32.5 knots
Range: 10,500 nautical miles at 15 knots
Crew: 1,799

# ANALYSIS AND CONCLUSION

The Baltimore class was the finest class of heavy cruiser that saw action during World War II. American designers had taken a good but imperfect design and made it into a well-balanced ship with good stability, good habitability for its expanded wartime crews, and room for wartime upgrades in antiaircraft weaponry and electronics. Most of all, the Baltimore-class ships possessed superior protection to any other wartime cruiser, as well as superior fighting power. The radar-guided 8in guns firing a heavy shell with good penetrative characteristics made the Baltimore class the most powerful heavy cruiser afloat. Their level of antiaircraft protection was clearly superior to that of any other wartime cruiser.

However, all of these advantages remained theoretical, not proven, since these fine ships never had an opportunity to show their full potential in combat. As shore-bombardment platforms, they were certainly adequate, and they proved themselves as good antiaircraft screening platforms.

The protection of these ships was also never severely tested, since they came to the Pacific late in the war. The most severe instance of damage due

to combat was when *Canberra* was hit by a single Japanese aircraft-launched torpedo on October 13, 1944. This flooded the two aft boiler rooms and both engine rooms, but the ship did not lose power in the two forward boiler rooms. The large size of the ship proved adequate to save it, but this was not unusual since Treaty cruisers also showed the ability to take a single torpedo hit, but usually sank when hit by two.

The Des Moines-class cruisers were fine ships in almost every way. They possessed excellent fire-control facilities, and the 8in rapid-fire gun proved reliable in service. However, they were terribly expensive. In 1945 dollars, they cost just over $48 million, compared to the cost of an Essex-class carrier of some $56.5 million.

Their volume of fire was impressive, but this attribute was wasted on shore-bombardment missions where a high rate of fire was not important. The protection of this class was superior to every other 8in cruiser ever built, since it combined fairly heavy armor with extensive compartmentation. Even if the ships were never tested in combat against their intended enemy, they did provide value to the American taxpayer since they served from the late 1940s into the 1970s.

The Alaska class never had a clear purpose since the ships they were built to counter – large Japanese cruisers – did not exist. Arriving in the Pacific in the last phases of World War II, the only role for them was as an antiaircraft escort for the fast carriers. Though they were fine ships in this role, they were essentially no better than any of the modern heavy cruisers. They were, in fact, a white elephant with no clear mission. If anything, they were a testament to the profligacy of the US Navy and its extravagant wartime construction plans.

They were designed for a very narrow mission: chasing down Japanese heavy cruisers. Had the Japanese ever employed their heavy cruisers independently, and had the *Alaska* ever come across one, it would certainly have overpowered it with its 12in guns and superior protection. However, just as the British had been tempted to use their early battlecruisers as capital ships in the battle line, it is much more likely that had the Imperial Navy posed a serious surface threat in 1945 when the Alaska-class ships entered service, the US Navy would have used its impressive large cruisers in a main-fleet action. Though the Alaska-class ships were well-protected for cruisers, their scale and the arrangement of their armor was still based on cruiser principles, and they would not have fared well against a real battleship.

This view from the bow aboard *Alaska* shows two of the ship's main battery turrets in June 1945. The two Alaska-class large cruisers were the only ships to employ this 12in gun. These never had the opportunity to engage their intended targets – Japanese surface ships – but they were used to bombard shore targets during World War II. (US Navy via Real War Photos)

They were expensive to build ($70 million in 1945 dollars), had an enormous crew of 2,200, and consumed fuel at an alarming rate. Their maneuverability was the worst of any large US Navy ship save the two Lexington-class carriers. Though large, they did not benefit from their size in terms of protection. The ships exhibited poor compartmentation, and, most glaringly, had no dedicated anti-torpedo protection. This made clear that they did not deserve to be considered as a battlecruiser.

# BIBLIOGRAPHY

Campbell, John, *Naval Weapons of World War Two*, Naval Institute Press, Annapolis, MD (2002)

Ewing, Steve, *American Cruisers of World War II*, Pictorial Histories Publishing Company, Missoula, MT (1989)

Friedman, Norman, *Naval Radar*, Conway Maritime Press, Greenwich (1981)

Friedman, Norman, *US Cruisers*, Naval Institute Press, Annapolis, MD (1984)

Friedman, Norman, *Naval Firepower*, Naval Institute Press, Annapolis, MD (2008)

Marriot, Leo, *Treaty Cruisers*, Pen and Sword Maritime, Barnsley (2005)

Terzibaschitsch, Stefan, *Cruisers of the US Navy 1922–1962*, Naval Institute Press, Annapolis, MD (1984)

Whitley, M. J., *Cruisers of World War Two*, Naval Institute Press, Annapolis, MD (1995)

Williams, David, *Naval Camouflage 1914–1945*, Naval Institute Press, Annapolis, MD (2001)

www.navweps.org

# INDEX

Page references in **bold** refer to photographs and captions. All US Navy ships listed are heavy cruisers unless otherwise stated.